No School Today?
A Home Spun Comic Strip Collection

By
Cristina Ramos-Payne

Writing the dedication for my first book is kind of like winning my first academy award. There are so many people I want to thank, and I'm afraid of forgetting someone. After all, who knows when I will have this experience again?

To my family
for believing in me, no matter how zany my schemes.

To the homeschoolers who visited my blogs
for inspiring me to continue past my original seven strips

To my friends
for encouraging me to gather my comics into a collection.

The first time I took pencil to paper and decided to cartoon my life, I never considered the possibility that my comics might eventually develop a life of their own. Although I use my own family as my primary source of inspiration, I have also been inspired by other homeschoolers I have met online and in person.

What I hope to achieve in offering my comics is to help others view our little world of homeschooling and perhaps see a little of themselves, whether they homeschool or not. I hope these snapshots of our life cause conversations to start and understanding to develop. I hope new homeschoolers start believing they can do this and veteran homeschoolers realize they are not alone in having meltdowns, burnouts, fears of inadequacy, and changes of attitudes about their homeschooling styles. The thing I love about homeschooling is that it is vibrant, pulsating, life learning that changes with the needs of each child. I can't imagine trying to teach my three—Marina, Chase and Sierra—in the same way, and I try to relate that dynamic educational style in my character counterpart, Jess Spinner.

Our lives change in the blink of an eye. My own children have grown much faster than their comic strip alter egos. Marina (Coral) is no longer a homeschooler, having started classes at a local college. Chase (Toby) is high school age and figuring out what direction he wants to take. Sierra (Aña) is my happy unschooler, a learning direction I never thought I would take when I started homeschooling so many years ago. My husband and extended family are still my strongest supporters on this journey. I am so grateful to them for giving me the courage to keep doing this through all of the growing pains, my children's as well as my own.

What you are about to read are the first two hundred Home Spun comic strips along with my thoughts, some reprinted from my blog and some brand new, because I am still learning and can't contain myself when an observation sets my mind to thinking. I hope you enjoy them.

May Your Life be Filled with Peace and Laughter,
Cristina Ramos-Payne

CAST OF CHARACTERS

Jess Spinner

Allen Spinner

Coral

Toby

Aña (not immediately appearing)

MOM! TOASTER KEEPS LAYING ON MY WRITING!
PURRR!
DON'T BLAME THE CAT! WORK AT A TABLE!
PURRR!

PLEASE DO YOUR WORK AT A TABLE!

WE'RE DONE! WAIT TILL MOM SEES!
MOM! COME LOOK AT OUR GREEK TEMPLE!
I THINK ATHENA'S A LITTLE TOO FUZZY...
PURRR!

I will point out now that I did not write these comics to belittle anyone's method of homeschooling. Just as every child learns in their own unique way, every homeschooling parent teaches in their own style. Some are more organized, some prefer hands-on activities, some pool their resources and set up co-ops. Add to that the different philosophical styles: classical, Charlotte Mason, project-based, Waldorf, child-led, Montessori, online schools, eclectic... the list goes on. We pick the style that is the right fit for our family and each of our children. That doesn't mean another family's choices are wrong. One of the greatest aspects of homeschooling is educational freedom. As parents and guardians of our children, we know best how to facilitate learning, or we figure it out from the kids, or we experiment with various techniques until we find the one that works for us.

I should not concern myself with teaching my children.
Whatever I do, they will learn.
Instead, I should focus on teaching myself:

How I respond to challenges.
How I express my beliefs.
How I view the world.
How I view myself.

Whatever I do, they will learn.

I didn't realize it at the time, but these early ideas of stealth teaching were my earliest experiments with unschooling. My oldest hated to be asked about what she learned, because she equated learning with sitting in the living room with pen, paper and book. Back then, I was new at homeschooling, and I worried about my responsibility to the school district. I tended to push hard, which led to frustration when my five year old couldn't sit for two hours straight as I drilled her on phonics and counting. I was a taskmaster, and it isn't surprising she didn't want to learn.

In searching for a better way, I found that we could relax more on walks. I figured out games to play along the way. We would count our steps from one street to the next. We would play games like find the nouns/verbs/adjectives. We joined a homeschooling nature class where the group went on hikes with a park ranger and learned about the natural world around them. We spent hours at various libraries. And my daughter learned so much it would spout out of her at different times. But you could never ask her directly, "What did you learn." In her mind, this wasn't learning. This was fun!

In our early years of homeschooling, I could never make an experiment work the way I intended. We had many lessons that ended with us brainstorming about why an experiment failed. Did we measure wrong? Did we forget a step? Was it too humid? Too cold? Did we forget to let Daddy know we wanted that mold? Did we leave the experiment where a cat could reach it?

As nice as it would be to have a successful experiment, my children learned a lot from our botched attempts. They learned how important it was to follow instructions carefully. They learned that even when you do everything correctly, there are sometimes variables we don't expect. Perhaps the air is too dry or the day is too cloudy. Maybe the battery we used wasn't fresh and maybe the seeds were old. Sometimes no matter what you do, the experiment doesn't work.

I hope they learned that when things go wrong, it isn't the end of the world. A lot of times, I will take it upon myself to do some research and discuss my procedure with others who have done a similar experiment. Part of the learning experience is figuring out how you can make it work next time. If the only thing they gleaned from our experiment was to be persistent and keep trying to figure out a challenging problem, then I have not failed.

"I have not failed. I've just found 10,000 ways that won't work."

~Thomas A. Edison

One of the most common responses I get when I tell people I homeschool is, "I could never do that!" Lucky for them, I'm not recruiting. And really, I don't know anyone who could teach every subject on every grade level. That's why homeschoolers are resourceful. We figure out where to look for answers. I know which relatives can help me with my weak points, like algebra. I know how to search for help online and at the library. By doing this, I'm not only helping my child to learn, I'm showing her how to research and find answers. No subject is intimidating if you can find a way to understand it.

My oldest learned to knit twice. The first time she learned from a library book we borrowed. I thought I would be able to learn right alongside her, but she quickly outpaced me. One stumbling block to her knitting was the cat, who kept stealing her knitting. The other was me. Because I didn't know a knit from a purl she didn't get farther than squares and rectangles and soon grew bored. Several years later, she took up the needles again, this time with a group of her friends. With this social motivation and the occasional help of a veteran knitter, she developed a skill that she will never forget.

Papier mâche is something I avoid doing too much in our house. There really isn't a neat way to do it. Creativity is messy! I pick splotches of dry paste off of the floor for days. The flour paste ferments because we are too busy to finish it in one week. Their models take days to dry because they used too much paste. Then I have to push the kids to finish because they lose interest. So why do it at all?

Because I always forget, so we do it again the following year.

One of the great freedoms of homeschooling is the ability to incorporate our traditions into our lessons. One of our traditions at Christmastime is the annual baking of the Aunt Kate cookies. These are rolled cookies that can take several family members hours to make. When we are down to the final scraps of dough, we finish with the amoeba or shapeless cookie. Thinking of ways to teach lessons with our traditions gives deeper meaning to learning.

Although I modeled Bea (Gramma) after my own grandma, Miguel is modeled after my dad. Marina was the first to call him Buelo, shortened from abuelo or grandfather. Growing up with two different cultural experiences for Christmas made life interesting! Puerto Ricans celebrate on "Little Christmas" (Epiphany) rather than on December 25. It did spread out the festivities and family visiting. I still celebrate across the entire twelve days of Christmas and I've added my mother's German tradition of hanging stockings on St. Nicholas Day. This helps children celebrate their mixed heritage, rather than focusing on one hectic day.

When Chase and Marina were younger, I was more traditional in my homeschooling methods. Everyone worked on math at the same time, with Marina off in the kitchen while I found ways to engage Chase. His dinosaur collection can be thanked for helping him figure out addition and subtraction. Unfortunately, it was also a distraction for Marina, who was beginning to have trouble with higher math concepts. I look at these comics and feel sad that I didn't have the tools I have today to help her through the bumpy parts. Ah well. We all live and learn. Homeschooling teaches us all. Back then I relied heavily on math adept extended family. These days we make use of online math resources and books and DVDs from the library. And I've gotten a lot better at math myself.

It's no fun to have a sick child in the house. You suffer with them, especially when your child is normally energetic and suddenly needs to take a long nap in the middle of the day. These are the times when I am most grateful I homeschool. I don't have to decide whether I can afford to take a day or find a sitter while my child is suffering. It also means he doesn't really miss class, since he can still learn, even if it means watching a DVD, listening to music or to a story, or reading or drawing in bed.

Thankfully, I have learned over the years of filing reports for my New York school district. I still get nervous about the quarterlies. It's that fear of judgment thing. My humbling experience in writing quarterly reports: you really don't have to write all that much. My father and other schoolteacher friends who would occasionally check my quarterlies reiterated teachers didn't write this much for their assessments. Of course, they had classes of 25+ students, but that's beside the point! The school only wants to know that you are following the home instruction plan you wrote and that you are meeting your goals. Keep it simple!

I had not realized at first that Marina had set up a museum for all of her science discoveries and art and history treasures. My mother would take her to museums all the time, so it really was no surprise that she would want her own. When her collection began to overwhelm her dresser top, I gave her a wooden box and helped her make a miniature museum with display stands. Supporting a child's creativity is so important. Having her own museum really helped her express what she learned in science and history. Playing museum curator made the lessons stay with her.

Meeting our falconer friend, Jim, was a thrill for my children. They love all animals and were eager to share their observations. Chase was five when we met Jim at the college where he worked. Chase was very into dinosaurs. I explained that we were seeing Jim to discuss birds, thinking Marina would ask more bird related questions. I didn't want him to interrupt with a hundred dinosaur facts. It turned out that Marina became incredibly shy and Chase was the one who asked all the questions regarding raptors!

It happens to all parents. There are nights when sleep is impossible, but we still have to figure out how to get ourselves out of bed after a night of disturbances and somehow function during the day. These are the times we need to go easy on ourselves. Traditional homeschoolers need to trust that the children won't leak intelligence if mom isn't hanging over them. Children can surprise us by taking their learning into their own hands. My older two were so set in a routine when they were younger and I was dealing with a restless baby, they often started their studies before I got up in the morning.

All kids are different. How often have you heard that? So simple, so often repeated, and yet so unheeded. Think of the standards our schools set. All children must learn the same things to graduate. Even I've been guilty of trying to use the same teaching techniques on Chase simply because they worked with Marina. Then I added Sierra and found that I needed to start anew for the third time. At least I don't get bored. For me, homeschooling has been an endless experiment of trying out different tools to satisfy each child's unique learning style.

HAVE YOU FINISHED PACKING FOR OUR TRIP TO PUERTO RICO, TOBY?
YEP! BUT I CAN'T CLOSE THIS.
LET ME SEE. MAYBE WE JUST NEED TO REFOLD...
TOBY, WHERE ARE YOUR CLOTHES?
THEY DIDN'T FIT!
MOM, DO YOU HAVE ROOM IN YOUR SUITCASE?

LADIES AND GENTLEMEN, WE ARE ON OUR FINAL APPROACH, WELCOME TO PUERTO RICO!
CLAP! CLAP!
CLAP! CLAP WOO!
CLAP CLAP
WHY IS EVERYONE CLAPPING?
¡ESOS SÍ SON DE AQUI! THE PUERTO RICANS APPLAUD WHEN THEY ARRIVE!
CLAP! CLAP!

DO YOU HEAR THAT SOUND? THOSE ARE THE COQUIS SINGING!
COQUI! COQUI!
COQUI! COQUI!
COQUIS ARE A PUERTO RICAN TREE FROG. LET'S GET SOME SLEEP AND WE CAN LOOK FOR THEM IN THE MORNING!
COQUI! COQUI!
YAWN!
COQUI! COQUI! COQU
WHEN DO THEY QUIET DOWN?
WHEN THE ROOSTERS WAKE UP!

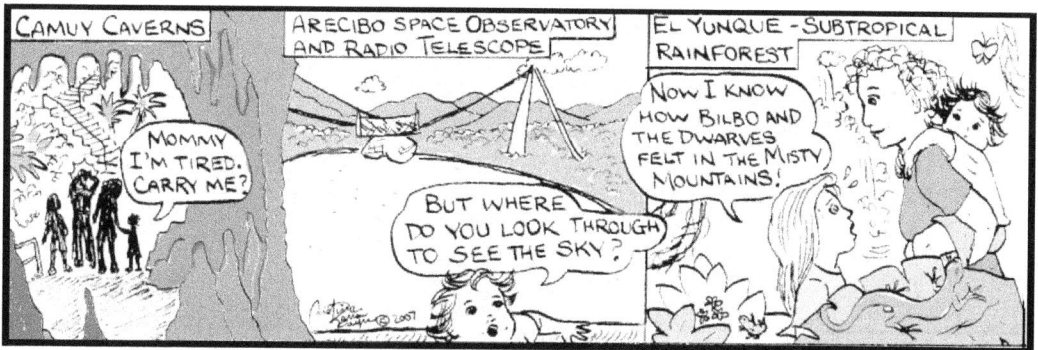

I first began to draw Home Spun when I had only two children. After I became pregnant for the third time, I set aside my ideas in a drawer and set my mind to figuring out how to homeschool two while tending to a baby. I still followed the classical model, albeit I had become very eclectic, especially after the busy Christmas season. When I finally allowed myself to return to my little strip and started posting it online, I knew I would eventually need to

add the third child. I promised myself I would do that when Sierra was old enough to notice she didn't have a character. I wanted the addition to be special, because she was my third child, just as I was the third of three. I even allowed her to name her character. That's a big deal for me. I love naming things. Years later, I know she doesn't really remember the experience, but that doesn't mean it wasn't important. It was very important. For me.

I would say one of the greatest challenges for modern homeschoolers is trying to spend time at home. Most of us would be better defined as carschoolers, since that is where we spend a good portion of our day. If I could give only one piece of advice to a new homeschooler, it would be this: Try to limit the number of activities your children do. Burning out from weeks of hectic living is no fun. You become irritable, lean on caffeinated beverages for support and are more susceptible to illness. Slow down! There will be many years to do all you want your children to do. Why use up all your energy before the end of your first year of homeschooling?

When we discuss homeschooling, it is often assumed that the primary home educator is the mother. I decided I wanted to make sure I represented the homeschooling father. The above comics are the result of talking with my friend and homeschooling father about some of the unique issues that faced him when he began his homeschooling journey. Since I wrote this, I've met many more fathers who are the primary home educators, as well as grandparents and other family members. The "home" in homeschooling is not just mom and the kids; it's a loving community of learning!

My husband gives a lot of support to our homeschooling lives. Not only does he bring home the steady paycheck, he also provides back up for me by helping our children with math and computer problems (his strengths), giving me breaks by taking the kids out or letting me have alone time, and by being my number one cheerleader when I start doubting myself. We make a good team. I think involving him in what we do has helped him feel more a part of the homeschooling experience.

We came up with this idea while reading a favorite mystery series by Elizabeth Peters. And yes, I am the slowest reader in the room, partially due to motherly distractions. We do enjoy reading and discussing our books together. Mysteries in particular are fun to pick apart. Everyone manages to notice different clues while reading.

Our approach for all favorite book series is the same. We take it chapter by chapter, trying to figure out what will happen, throwing out theories and opinions. Reading really brings us together.

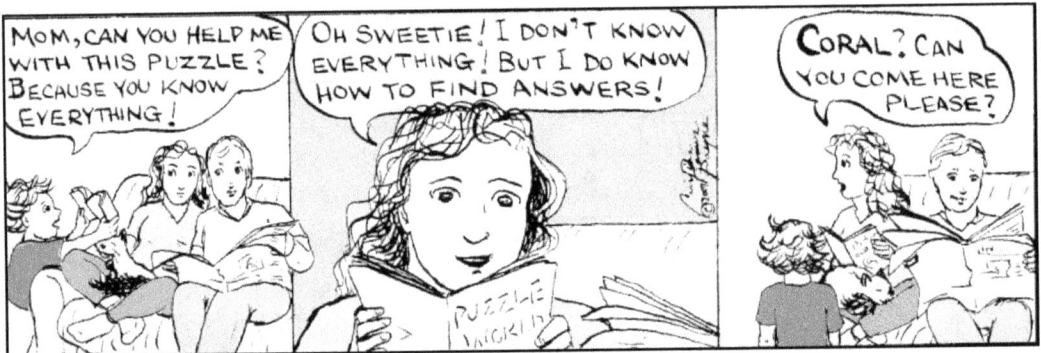

There was a time when my kids thought I knew everything. I think it was the few minutes right before they learned how to read. Then came the corrections. Suddenly, the mouse was a shrew. Anyone can see that it's a centipede, not a millipede. No, Mom, you forgot about (insert middle of story that I left out). Yes, I knew that, it was in the newspaper yesterday. That wasn't what happened in the movie/book/television show. What Shakespeare REALLY meant was...

OK, I threw that last one in, but I'm sure it will eventually happen. So just who's homeschooling whom?

My youngest child was born at home. We kidded that we do everything at home, why not have the baby there too? Many people were uncertain when we decided to do this. What if something went wrong? Well, just as with everything else in life, we would deal with problems as they came up. Just as with homeschooling, it was something I had to try, at least once. And it was a wonderful experience, one that I believe Chase and Marina will not soon forget.

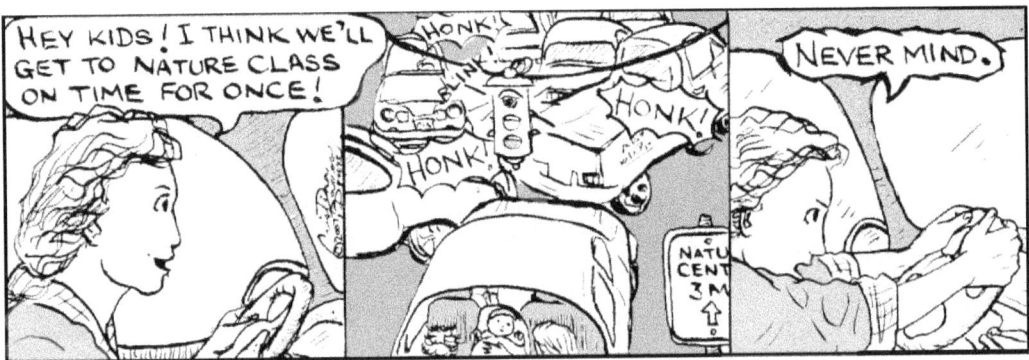

There is a slight error in the comic above. I'm not right-handed. And I found this is a vital observation when you are teaching your child to write. Being a visual learner, he tried to copy what I did exactly, putting the pencil in his left hand. He's not left-handed.

Panel 1: WHEN DO YOU DO YOUR HOMESCHOOL WORK, CORAL?

(book reads: OUR FAITH)

Panel 2: I START AFTER I GET UP AND HAVE BREAKFAST.

Panel 3: I WOULDN'T GET UP UNTIL NOON!

Panel 4: CAN YOU EAT OR DRINK ANYTHING WHILE YOU WORK?

Panel 5: SURE!

Panel 6: YOU ARE SO LUCKY YOU HOMESCHOOL! OKAY... ???

Panel 7: THE KIDS AT RELIGIOUS ED. CLASS WERE ASKING ABOUT HOMESCHOOLING.

Panel 8: IT'S ALWAYS THE SAME QUESTIONS! IT'S SO BORING!

Panel 9: NO ONE EVER ASKS ME WHAT I'M STUDYING!

In my opinion, two resources that make homeschooling possible for any family are computers and a good public library. Between the resources available online and the books and materials available at the library or through inter-library loan, it is possible to educate your children on a shoestring budget. A library card is usually free. Instead of buying canned curricula, invest in a good computer system with high speed internet. With these tools, I have all I need to access a wealth of information.

NOW THINK OF AN ANIMAL TO WRITE A POEM ABOUT.

I HAVE ONE!

LET'S SEE TOBY!

Komodo dragon
Komodo dragon
Why do you have
bacterea in yore
drool Why cant
you clime on a
stool how big

"COME UNTO THESE YELLOW SANDS" IS A POEM FROM "THE TEMPEST." SHAKESPEARE INVITES US IN WITH SOUNDS AND FESTIVE IMAGERY.

ROSE WHERE DID YOU GET THE RED?

MY POEM IS ABOUT A LAND IN THE SKY!

MINE IS ABOUT A LAND OF DRAGONS, MONSTERS AND DINOSAURS.

IT'S SO EASY TO TELL THEM APART!

THIS POEM IS SO BEAUTIFUL CORAL!

I WANT TO ENTER IT IN THE TOWN POETRY CONTEST!

NO!

WHAT IF I WON? I WOULD HAVE TO READ IT!

When I first started Home Spun comics, I could not imagine reaching twenty strips, let alone two hundred. As any mom, I was focused on simply making it through the day and pushing my own interests to one side. It is easy to forget that as wonderful and important as it is to be self-sacrificing, we are also a role model to our children. I want them to see me loving and taking care of them, but I also want them to see that I love and take care of myself. My comic strip and blog became the creative outlet I needed to keep myself sane through my early years of homeschooling and mothering. I don't devote as many hours as I would like to it. My family will always come first in my life. But I do manage to devote a few hours each week to my art and writing. It makes me happy. When I am happy, I can tackle the challenges that arise daily with calm. I'm not perfect. I still lose my temper from time to time and sometimes a good cry helps release an unusual amount of stress. But in my drawings and words I can find the peace and laughter in my life and use it for support.

About the Author

Cristina Ramos-Payne never imagined all the twists and turns her life would take leading her to write about herself in the third person. She grew up eating good Bronx pizza and taking frequent trips to the New York Botanical Garden and the Bronx Zoo. She attended the High School of Art and Design and completely turned her back on her art to pursue a degree in psychology from Lehman College. She learned to juggle and met her husband at a juggling club meeting in the West Village. As of this writing, they have been happily married for twenty years. She found work as a facepainter, a street performer, a teaching assistant and a gymnastics and circus arts instructor. Cristina homeschooled her three children from the beginning, and continues homeschooling the younger two while ferrying the oldest back and forth to community college. She began writing her comics as a creative outlet. She always thought she took herself too seriously, so finding the humor in her life was a survival tactic. This led to blogging. She now writes comics and articles on homeschooling and family life at her blog, Home Spun Juggling. Visit her online at http://jugglingpaynes.blogspot.com

www.ingramcontent.com/pod-product-compliance
Lightning Source LLC
Chambersburg PA
CBHW081636040426
42449CB00014B/3337